W9-AXZ-017

Bourne to Luv

A Collection of Beautifully Crafted Poetry

by
Hazel "Bourne" Carter

BOURNE TO LUV

ISBN: 978-0-692-94217-8

Copyright © 2017 by Hazel Bourne

All rights reserved. No part of this book may be reproduced or transmitted in any form or by any means without written permission from the author.

Published by Gospel Inks

www.gospelinks.com

407-912-1493

Cover artwork © 2017 by Kelvin Hamilton Bourne

Printed in the United States of America

About The Poet

Hello! My name is Jennifer Hazel Bourne. Carter is my married name. I am fondly known by my middle name, Hazel. I am what you would call a real "NUT"- humorous and spontaneous. I was born in a little village called Palo Seco on the beautiful island of Trinidad to my parents, Cynthia Umilta & Jacob Eliezer Bourne who had seven children together, of which I am the sixth. They are Desmond, Gloria, Faith, Kelvin, Sherma, and Andy. I later became the sister of Abdon Mason, the present Mayor of Point Fortin, Trinidad, and Brenda and Bertrand by my Dad who is the father of ten amazing children. I am also the proud mom of Christian Nathaniel Carter who is a blessing to me from God.

Although I was born in Palo Seco, I grew up in the town of Tunapuna where I attended primary and secondary school and became a friend to many. I wrote my first poem when I was in primary school in Standard 3B -Mr. Ash's class. My poem was so raw and unpolished that it angered an Indian girl I used to bully. I ended up in a canal full of dirty water. After secondary school I worked as a cashier at HILO Food stores and later as a temporary clerical clerk at the Ministry of Education until I migrated to the USA.

I started writing poems full scale at my church, International Christian Center, when I was given the opportunity to do the announcements and birthday greetings. I soon transformed the announcements and birthday greetings by adding my own poetic flair and performance to it. Since then, I have written seventy poems, sixty-eight of which are contained in this book.

I am so thankful to God for allowing me to put my short stories into poetry form. This poor girl who grew up in a little village had a dream, not knowing it could be a reality. I put my thoughts about things I have experienced or heard of into poetry. I like humor, so I added a little of it to some poems depending on the topic.

On April 15th 2017, I shared my poems with friends and family in an event I called A TIME 2T. It was well received. I then decided that it was time to put them all in a book so that others could enjoy them.

I pray that this book reaches the world. I believe that there is a poem in this book that each person can relate to. I thank you for reading.

Acknowledgements

First, I would like to thank the Almighty God for making me unique,
and for depositing this gift in me

To my wonderful son, Christian Nathaniel Carter,
you are a gift from God

To my Amazing mother, Cynthia Umilta Bourne. I miss you
tremendously. You did a great job being the **best** Mom.

To my dad Jacob Bourne-thank you Daddy,
first for giving me the gift of life

To my nine wonderful humorous, humorous siblings:
Desmond, Gloria, and Faith (thanks for always having my back).

Kelvin -thank you for giving me permission to use your painting of our
home for the cover of my book.

Sherma it is because of you that I am where I am today.
Thank you so much.

Andy, Abdon, Brenda and Bertrand. I'm so glad to be your sister.

For believing in me, the LOVE of my life Mr. Junior Wilson.
Thanks for being my ROCK

Thank you Pastor Rojas, Uncle Cecil Rocke, Carlene Green, Marlene
Delamothe-Bourne, Odette Octaville, Valerie Bennett, Theresa
Fraser, Michelle Borel-thanks girl for pushing me, Trudy Rojas,
Shirma Gomez, Ray J, Jennifer Ochoa, Verika and many others, who
stood on the side line and cheered me on. You know who you are.

Thank you so much

My best friends Alicia Phillip and Joseph Martinez (who has departed), I wish you were here to share this moment.

I miss you. RIP

Dedication

I dedicate this book to
My Wonderful Son
Christian Nathaniel Carter

Contents

About Hazel

Hazel's Birthday Poem

I wrote this poem, because I'm so happy
Because I was born on August 20th, 1963
I am a mother, sister, cousin and friend
I promise to serve the Lord, till the end

I was born in Palo Seco, Trinidad
My early years, life was very hard
I look back from where God has brought me from
I pledge to smile daily, and not wear a frown

I cried many months when my first child died
I couldn't understand, and kept asking God "why"
He later blessed me, with a handsome son
Who makes me talk a lot, and that's not sometimes fun

I accepted the Lord in 1993
Every day, God is so good to me
I'll continue to dye my hair, as long as I can see,
Because grey hair, does not look too pretty on me

I migrated to America, in January "96"
In "09", was hospitalized, because I got very sick
I greatly appreciate life, after that heart attack
Living it to the fullest, with no turning back

Seems like only yesterday, I was 21
Hanging out with me, you are sure to have fun
I am proud of my age, I thank God everyday
For blessing my family and I, in so many ways

I'm misunderstood at times by so many
Because I speak my mind, ask my family
What you see, is what you get
Hazel is not trying to be like the rest

Hey, if you want a good joke, you can consider me,
Even though the most mail I get now, is from AARP
Since "98" I am a proud member, of ICC
Where the motto is "where everybody is somebody"

My First Child

Hearing, "you are pregnant" was one of the happiest days of my life.
I'm going to be a mother, 16 months after being a wife.
My imagination was going crazy, how would you look
On being a new mother, I read every book.

I did everything to ensure that you were growing healthy
Prenatal care at Mt. Hope hospital was a trip I made weekly
You were going to be beautiful, that I know for sure
I smile to myself, closing your decorated bedroom door.

I had to be rushed to the hospital, you were three weeks early
I knew pretty soon my baby will be calling me mommy
At 9 pm before the anesthesiologist put me to sleep
I felt you move, that feeling was so very sweet.

I kept asking the nurses what baby I had
They said "relax" and that made me feel somewhat glad
I was in pain, my stomach felt butchered
I wanted to know about my baby and when we would
be discharged
October 27th 1991, I was excited with no regrets
The next morning I heard words, I'll never forget
The doctor told me my baby girl had died
Through my tears and loud scream, I kept asking "why"

Why is this man with a white shirt and stethoscope hurting me?
His words made me sad, angry and unhappy
The night before, my baby was alive
Now he's telling me, that she lived a few hours then died

I saw Curise Hazel, wrapped in brown paper
in the hospital mortuary
There laid the child that grew in my belly
Tears rolling down my eyes, I didn't want to leave her
She's the baby I wanted, my precious daughter.

No words from my family and friends could have comforted me
I did everything right, how could this be
The tears never stopped flowing, that first year was the hardest.
Trying to stay positive and move on, I couldn't comprehend it
Today almost 26 years later, I still think of my baby
Who I will never see her graduate from college or even get married

I now believe, I had this experience so I could share with others
With some grieving fathers and heartbroken mothers
You do not know the pain I felt since you didn't walk in my shoes
But a word to encourage another family, that for sure I can do.

9/17/16

Ward 11 -MHTA

On ward eleven the MHTA work as a team
Whether we are doing fresh air, or vending machine
Ricketts, Sam , Jane and Carter are the fantastic four
You know we mean business, as you walk through the door

Twenty four seven, our job is about patient care
We are efficient and reliable when we are there
We do our job happily and to the best of our ability
Going out of our way taking care of everybody

The staff knows their job and what they are doing
Jane is considered the energizer, she is always moving
While loud mouth Ricketts, really holds things down
Making the job so much easier, when things go wrong
Yes grey beard Ricketts is very dependable
Even though he makes fun of Jane, Sam and Hazel

Bow legged Sam does a great job doing the environment search
His kindness also shows when he donates lots of pants,
shoes and shirts
Carter likes updating the books, ensuring there's enough
extra copies
Also taking care rolling the towels , making them nice and fancy

Recently two new workers joined our bunch, indeed it's a pleasure
They seem to be happy, as we all work together
With the needs of the patients as our number one priority
We will continue to do our best to keep our surroundings safely
2/8/17-3:30am

Life Can Be So Funny

Bad

I like you very much
Of course I like you very much
But I hate when your teeth you don't brush
Don't let your breath blow others away
Remember to brush your teeth everyday
If out of the blue I offer you a mint
It's only a decent way of saying" I care," what do you think?

Be True To Yourself

What you see, isn't always what you think
People hide their truth, under those fancy clothes and bling
If the authentic person becomes visible to others
They wouldn't believe the shell was only a cover

Some people shop at local convenient stores
To their friends, such places are for the poor
They would rather put their paid purchases
in a different store bag
Just to fool others, with that camouflage

There are handbags that are very cheap
One can get a good bargain from a vendor on the street
Why spend hundreds of dollars on a bag that is name brand
Inside your wallet is empty, while holding that Michael Kors
on your right hand
You really don't need to go on that trip with friends
Your rent is less than it costs for that weekend

You can put yourself together nicely and no one can tell
Clearance rack is responsible for many of us looking well
Some folks' outfits, from head to toe can cost fifty dollars
While their friends choose to shop at fancy, "Lord & Taylor"
When you go out, folks call you a trendsetter
Even though you don't buy Gucci, Guess or even Prada.
Take a page from my simple book
It's not the cheap price you pay, but how you look

Ladies and gentlemen, don't shop at places you can't afford
Then on your knees you asking help from the Lord
Don't allow your bill payments to be late
Trying to impress others with purchases you make

What you are doing is hurting yourself
Picking up expensive items off high end shelves
You can't afford that lifestyle, "leave it alone"
Shop at Burlington, Pretty Girl or Rainbow
They have the same styles as Macy's and Bloomingdales
At times you get better bargains when on sale

Don't try to fit in, you have your mold
Wear your "No Name" items proud and bold
Don't dress and try to be like your associates
Their credit card bills have them stressed, make no mistake
Why try to be like the rest
Don't you know "no man can curse who God has blessed"
Please don't hang your hat higher than you can reach
Stop being camouflage as you walk the street.

Wednesday October 26-11 am

Ladies & High Heels

Life is good, life is sweet
Ladies, those shoes we wear are hurting and damaging our feet.
Step after step, there is excruciating pain, walking on the street
Shoes feel comfortable in the store, but after we purchase them
They make you grind your teeth.

Ladies, not every shoe we like , we must buy
Because some cause us real pain, deep down inside
Yet we refuse to take them off,
Even though our toes are on fire
While every footstep we take, makes us squint and perspire.

Daily I see women wearing these high, high shoes
The way they walk, you can imagine the pain they are going through.
They walk very slowly and with a little bend
Gladly stopping to answer a call, or a text somebody send.

Some ladies have to stop walking suddenly, to ease
their foot discomfort
To them, they don't look cute when the shoe heels are very short
Even though these high heels give them great pain
They go back and buy the same eight inch shoe,
over and over again.

Ladies if you know you cannot walk in these high heel shoes,
please don't buy them
Because later on, your feet will have plenty of problems
Women look very elegant when they can step assertively in their shoe
With such comfort, long movement and dancing are some things
they can do.

If you cannot walk in the shoes, let me reiterate, leave them alone
It makes no sense you are limping , from the time you leave home.
4/16/17-10.30 pm

Life is a Journey

Unpredictable
Life's Sudden Changes

When the days are lonely
it seems so long
And all the DJ does is play
those sad, sad songs
She doesn't know how long
the ache will last
But knows one day,
"this too shall pass"

It was only yesterday
they were happy as could be
Everyone said she had
the perfect family
A mother and father who
loved their children
Making sure they spend
quality time, every weekend

No one knows what the future holds
Whether it is hot like summer or the blast of winter's cold
The final touches were made to their beautiful new home
She didn't know tomorrow, in that big house, she'll be all alone

She awoke in the hospital, thinking it must be a dream
"This tragedy didn't happen to me ", she loudly screamed
Why didn't that driver stop at the red light
Seeing him speeding towards us, was a terrible fright

Weeks turn into months, but the pain remains fresh
She lost her whole family, how could she say she's blessed
The love they shared, will forever live in her heart
Not even death can take it away, or keep their love apart
May 5th 2014-2pm

Devices

What is going on in this society?
Has everyone lost their minds and gone crazy?
No longer are people talking to each other
The new way of communication is through a finger.

I entered a car on the train, heading to the city
Not one single head raised up to look at me
I counted 16 people sitting in that car
All heads were bowed, staring at their iPad and cellular

The man in blue must have read something funny
While the toddler in a stroller, wanted the attention
from the young lady.
He kept grabbing her hands, but she was busy texting
She quickly stuffed the pacifier in his mouth,
while grumbling something

I noticed the fingers of another passenger , moving fast
like if in a race.
Next to him, the old lady on the left, kept a composed
look on her face.
Even the group that came in, no one talked to each other
Because in their hands they held the mighty cellular

The one who invented these devices should take the blame
For me having problems exiting the now crowded train
Many, even while standing, were busy looking at their screen texting
and playing
Refusing to move aside or to even look at their surroundings

What is our once beautiful world coming to?
As parents, we have given our kids other things to do.

In 20 years from now, how will the generation be?
No one will be talking or thinking of climbing a tree

Reading a book and turning the actual pages is a thing of the past
Playing in the park with other children will not last
We are losing each other because of these smart devices
That is doing everything for us, oh the advantage and disadvantages

The cellular has taken over
Nobody is sitting and talking to each other
To get your loved one's attention you have to send them a text
Families are no longer having dinner together, I wonder what's next

1/12/17

Dilemma of An Addict

She looked at him, as he walked through the door,
He promised, he would not go there any more
She took his hands and asked him why
He said he needed help and started to cry
Many mornings he would leave home early for work
But will go there first, that's not a joke.
He knows he has to stop before it's too late
It could destroy his marriage, make no mistake

He got excited but ended up losing all very quickly
He is close to winning, and needs more money desperately
He immediately rushes to the nearest ATM
Praying he wouldn't have to visit it again
He is thankful; he alone sees the monthly bank statement
Explaining the numerous cash removal to his wife
would cause a big argument
When he's there he wonders why he gets this feeling of euphoria
Because when sitting by the machine, nothing else matters
He doesn't stop to eat or use the bathroom
He looks at his watch and knows he has to leave soon

He wants to leave the machine but is scared to walk away
Because he invested so much money in it that day
He will hate for someone to come after and win the jackpot
He will be very upset and freeze on the spot
He remembered the day he lied and said was meeting a friend
Most people don't know addicts lie, all the way, to the end
They tell you they are some place, but they are not.
If others know his truth, he will be embarrassed to the gut.

His savings account is now empty, the last hundred dollars
he withdraw

He can get out this, there must be a cure
His credit cards are all up to the max,
It was so easy getting cash advance in a flash

"Jesus, I need help", he cried out loud
He cannot request a loan from friends, he's way too proud.
His mortgage is late, so are his other payments.
How will he make tomorrow, he even borrowed from his retirement.
He has to stop going to the various casino
Besides his wife, he's embarrassed, no one else could know
The next few days will be a test of his faith
For total recovery, this young man can't wait.

On the other side of town, she tells her sister her kids are sick
Once she mentions them, she knows that will do the trick
She needs to get high, no matter what
Using her children, is the last excuse she's got
The eighty dollars she received will keep her happy a tad bit
This vice has destroyed her once beautiful relationship.
She lied, stole and borrowed, just to maintain her
drug habit
Selling her furniture, jewelry, body, and even her winter jackets
The other family members are tired of giving her chances
Only God can turn things around, in spite of her circumstances.

Addiction is real, it's a habit that invades your being, your very soul
Drugs, Cigarettes, Sex, Gambling or *Alcohol* some can't say **NO**
This is prevalent not only here in America, but all over the world
It's sad looking at some faces of once beautiful man,
women boy or girl
Thankfully there are Rehab centers available 24/7,
They are just a call away
There is help for you, make that move, get help TODAY
                    9/17/16- 9 pm

Behind Closed Doors

After eight hours, she is glad to leave work.
But when she gets home, there's so much hurt.
She cannot get there, no later than four
Otherwise, it's chaos and drama, behind closed doors.

Around their friends, they are always happy and smiling
Deep down inside, they don't know, she feels like crying
When she doesn't answer him, she is hit to the floor
They don't know she suffering, behind closed doors

Everyone says, they are a perfect couple
As they drink beer from a glass, never the bottle
Many times she says to herself," I'm not taking it no more"
God alone knows her pain, behind closed doors.

Only both of them know the truth about the abuse
Leaving him, and the kids, she is so confused
She's got to get away, that she knows for sure
There is no peace and love, behind closed doors.

There are many nights, of heartache and anguish
Others really don't know, of their real relationship.
She wonders if leaving him would be the cure.
She feels she can't survive another day, behind closed doors.

She sometimes sits and stares into oblivion.
Thinking of her so called, happy union
She wears designer's clothes, yes that is true
Under her Gucci glasses, her eyes are black and blue,
His words are no longer sweet, they're like a roar
When he kicks and beats her, behind closed doors.

Her envious neighbors, don't know the pain she feels inside
Her life is a fake that she will not deny
Verbal, mental and physical abuse, all three she endures
In her beautiful mansion, behind closed doors.
      December 10th 2013

Words

Words spoken can never be returned
It can cause one to smile and another one to hurt
Before you say something demeaning, think of the effects
Because hurtful words can make someone very upset

Share a word instead that will lift another up
Motivating a person, you'll see, it doesn't cost a lot
Speak about someone as if they are standing right there with you
Let your words be encouraging, helpful and true
1/23/17

Our Health

When we put an enormous amount of food on our plate
That is responsible for us gaining a lot weight
Which creeps up on us very quickly
and that, none of us appreciate .
Most of us have a hearty appetite for a scrumptious meal
But after consuming plenty, we dislike the uncomfortable
way we feel

Quite a lot of us, want to remain nice and slim
But make so many excuses,why we cannot go to the gym.
Feeling and looking good comes with responsibility
I can't do it for you, neither can you do it for me.
However if we work at motivating one another
We can start walking, then running and become healthier.

Almost everything we want, comes after lots
of saving and sacrifices
For example, a nice home, car, good education,
And travelling , they are all very expensive.
We cannot allow ourselves to become overweight or obese
Because this could lead to high blood pressure, stroke,
knee problems, heart attack and diabetes.
If we want to live a long healthier life
Before you eat that big plate full, let us please think twice.

May 2017

Family Always

My Son Christian

I am so happy you are my child
I call you my miracle and here is why
You were placed in the neonatal ward for special observation
Because at the time of your birth, I developed complications.

After forty eight hours , you improved and they placed you with me
It was a beautiful feeling and I was very happy
That feeling was short lived and fear took over
You developed jaundice and had to be placed in an incubator .

I watched and fed you in that room for three long days.
Nothing I did, made the tears go away.
I prayed and I cried, I cried and I prayed
As a new mom, I couldn't imagine what could take the worry away.

One week after you were born, finally we took you home
Holding you in my arms, I didn't want to let you go
I didn't want you to sleep in your fully decorated room
I wanted to be near you, so I broke my mother's rule.

As the days turned quickly into weeks,
You were growing healthy and you were chubby and sweet
The months flew by and you celebrated your first birthday
You made us laugh as you impersonated the way I pray.

We migrated to America when you were only sixteen months old.
In a blizzard that January , the place was freezing cold
However honey, you so quickly adjusted to the different life
and the weather
You happily played in the snow or swung in the park
for the hot summer.

The years passed by very fast and already you are in your twenties
I don't feel a day over 25, so how could this be.
Christian Nathaniel you are indeed (my gift from God)
Even if you make me upset, you'll always be my baby boy
With much love from your mother, you are my PRIDE & JOY.
Christian --- Christ like
Nathaniel---Gift from God

5/30/17-1:45 am

Faith (50th Birthday)

On December fourth,
fifty years ago
Smokey and Cynthia,
had their third baby to show
Faith Ann Marie Bourne
is her name
If you don't love her,
it would be a shame.

She is loved by her four
beautiful sisters
And appreciated by her five
handsome brothers

Faith is a mother of three adorable kids
Who gave her four grandchildren , before she could wink.

If you were here when she turned forty
You would remember, it was an awesome party
She decided from then to celebrate every single year
At her humble home, or in this basement right here

Yes, she came from a pretty long way
But look how good, she is looking today
Watching her now you will never tell
Even though back then, she thought, poverty was hell

She is very happy to reach this milestone ,
Because things were very tough, growing up back home
Coming to America has made her strong
In the heart of many, that's where she belongs

Faith she is called, by her family
To her New York friends, she is just, Ann Marie
A mother, grandmother, sister, cousin and friend.
We all wish you another 50 years, again and again.

I Miss You Mom

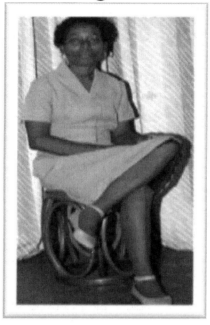

There is no one you can be compared to
You stood strong with the physical abuse you've been through
A mother of seven, you loved us dearly
I so miss hearing you call me "HAZEE"

A beautiful mixed breed woman, I call mammy
Sharing what she had with strangers was always so easy
As I grew older I sometimes called you CYNTIE
But couldn't do so in front of any body

You had a way of fixing your face, when I did something wrong
For sure it wasn't a smile, yet it wasn't a frown
It was a look that made me always shiver
Cause I know a "cut tail" was coming after

You never hesitated to tell me you love me
When I came first in test, Mom you shared the news proudly
For all of us you wanted the best
Reminding us we should never settle for less

I miss you because you were my mammy
Raising me alone with the absence of daddy
Looking back I wondered how
You never stressed neither did you fuss
The things you embraced, others would have cuss

I miss you because up to April 22nd, 2004
you were a phone call away
I remember the pain I felt when you died that day
The tears still blind my eyes thinking of you
Rolling down my cheeks and sticking to my pillow like glue

Mammy one day we will meet again
You were a mother right down to the end
Cynthia Umilta Bourne I know you are looking over me
Keeping me motivated appreciative and constantly happy.

9/18/16.11 am
The eve of mom's 80th birthday

Kelvin Hamilton Bourne

Kelvin Bourne is one of my brothers
His unique style, makes him different,
from the others,
We are all from the wonderful Bourne family,
And we love each other, as everyone could see

In 1975 he came to America
Along with his little brother and sister Sherma
He loves his life, and he is looking good,
A lot of times, he's misunderstood

When you talk about funny, Kelvin is number one
To Cynthia and Smokey, he is their second son.
When he is around, you can't help but laugh,
He won a comedy competition, he couldn't come last.

Loving and supporting him is his wife Marlene
His friend, his companion, she is his queen
They fit together like a hand in glove
Their home is blessed and is filled with love

After 34 years living in America
His desire was to succeed and not be a failure
Kelvin wanted to become an American citizen
But was afraid, he thought it may never happen

After much convincing, he took up the task
It was not easy, anyone could ask
On October 29th, his dream finally came through
He can now fly back home, "God, we thank you"

The death of our parents, hit him really hard,
Just talking about them, makes him very sad.
When he travels to Trinidad, he will finally see,
Where they laid to rest, our sweet mother, Cynthie

With paint brush in hand, he's so creative
Always happy to be around his relatives
A husband, father, brother, cousin, and friend
We are happy for you, Kelvin, you are a gem

10/27/09

The Solid Rock

From Sheriff Street, in beautiful Tunapuna,
Cecil Uban Rocke migrated to America
He is my dearly departed mother's baby brother
Who was born many, years ago, on the 12th of October
In Trinidad he stood watch at Golden Grove Prison as a prison officer
Today at New fellowship Missionary Baptist Church (MBC),
he is the pastor

At the New Testament church, he answered to the call of God,
Over 40 years, uncle Cecil has been serving the Lord.
In that church, he sat, under the late, Pastor, Ivan Patterson,
Where he became a Sunday School teacher and was loved for
his Bible lesson

He is good at singing, but never made a record
Uncle Cecil's desire always is "to wait on the Lord"
There are a lot of things I bring up, he can't remember
I think I'll have to send him a few bottles of Ginkoba

As a youth, when I asked him to sponsor me a cinema show
Uncle Cecil never frowned, quarrelled or told me NO
He would always leave some of his nice, tasty food for me
Because I would ask first, before my cousins Jennifer and Judy
When my dad couldn't be there, Uncle Cecil was the one
to give me away
He made sure I was happy and smiling on my wedding day.

In June 1977 he got married to vivacious Marva
I thank God for blessing and keeping this union, many years later.
They have a handsome son and a gorgeous granddaughter,
Sharing happy memories they will always remember.
Uncle Cecil personifies the word Christ like
He is kind, loving and takes good care of his wife
He is concerned about people and their wellbeing
Lending a helping hand often, to the lost and suffering.

Before you stands this exceptional man, I'm proud to call my uncle
To some he's a friend, pastor, or just a wonderful person to know
Of all his nieces, His favorite is, my sister Faith.
To Marva he is her husband, best friend and soulmate
Almost two years ago he started this powerful ministry
Not only is he a good man, Cecil Rocke is also a Trini
Faith and I are so happy to be here at New Fellowship MBC
Thanks for the warm welcome we received from everybody

Uncle Cecil, God has kept you for over 40 years
He'll do it again, so have no fear
You've sat and passed the entire test
God isn't finished with you yet.
Your desire is to see the empty seats full
As you remain committed to God, we know soon they would
Weeping may endure, it is written, for a night,
Joy is coming, pastor, everything will be alright

Cecil Urban Rocke, I salute you
As God's work, you continue to do
God is good, He is good all the time
Continue my uncle , to shine, shine, shine.
Thursday October 6th 2016

Rupert Wilson

Rupert Wilson , was a man I was honored to call Dad
When I heard he was rushed to Down State Hospital
I felt very sad
I dropped what I was doing and got to the hospital quickly
Only to be told he passed away, by the nurse on duty.
I couldn't comprehend, for it was only a few hours we had spoken
Dad was laughing and talking, how could this happen.

From our first meeting, I noticed he was a
 "No Nonsense, Straightforward Man"
I gave him the utmost respect that day he shook my hand
He was a man of few words, he didn't say much
But if you tried to take his picture, he sure made a fuss

Dad enjoyed the many stories, I shared with him at home
Surprising even Junior , when our conversation
lasted longer on the phone.
I can still hear his laughter when I told him something funny
He laughed till he cried, he thought I was crazy.

The night before his passing , his voice was very strong
We chatted a little , I was at work and couldn't stay long
He made sure and told me "to reach home safe"
Not knowing we will never again see each other's face

One week before he was called home ,we sat watching television
A few memories of the past, he was happy to mention
Dad's memory was sharp as if he drank plenty Ginkoba
Folks his age and younger, don't have the ability to remember

Hearing "Your Dad Lived A Full Life" is no comfort to the
loved ones
Don't matter our parents' age, we are sad when they are gone
I can't believe we are saying goodbye to Dad today
In the hearts of many, forever he will stay
Dad we bid you farewell as we say our final goodbye
Of course we will miss you, that's why we cry
Franklin, Herbert, Von, Joy and Junior will all remember
The sacrifice you made, you were indeed their hero and father
November 10th 2016 -10pm

Trini Style

Our America Story

Most of us, did almost anything to come to America
Lining up for hours by the US embassy, just to get that visa,
Selling out everything we worked very hard to get
We are going to America, yes our mind is set
Our vision of this place is much better in fantasy,
What we do here to survive is a surprising reality
Getting to where we want to be is a rocky journey
Pay attention fully, as you listen to our America story

Because of the switch, we are faced with a big culture shock
Instead of saying "in between street", in New York,
they are called blocks
Plus we can no longer keep our doors opened,
they are always locked
"Doo Doo", in Trinidad, is a term of endearment
Call someone that here, will cause a BIG Argument
A lot of times we get depressed, and homesick
For me, I can tell you, praying was the only trick

We all came to this land, for a much better life
But end up sometimes working, for a horrible husband or wife
Families back home think, we are getting things really easy.
That is so untrue, try working as a housekeeper, handyman
or a nanny.

Most times we have to get to the live in job, on a Sunday night.
Thinking of our family back home, holding back tears
at times, is a fight.
We make so many sacrifices, to provide for our children
Who are depending on us, as we pack another barrel to send.

Nannies take the kids to school, doctor visit, and
other activities,
Yet still we to have to prepare nutritious meals,
for them to eat.
Walking the kids in very cold weather, is a must,
To keep your job, you just can't make a fuss
Some employers really think we are magicians
Asking us to do the impossible, without full compensation.
They love to tell us, that we are part of the family,
But the unfair way they treat us, how could that be
Because, when introducing us to their friends,
it's "meet my nanny"

It's not easy working as a housekeeper also
Somehow your workload just continues to grow and grow.
When you stand up for your rights, they want to fire you
With no green card, you sometimes don't know what to do.
You have to run errands, wash, clean, and cook
At nights you're so tired, you can't even read a book
Before Facebook, and Tango, communication back home
was via phone cards
Not seeing your own kids grow up is so very hard.

On leaving work Friday night, you rush to get your stuff done
Sometimes missing out on a backyard lime and summer fun
Saving every cent you have, to get a reputable lawyer
To help get that mighty green card, to visit your children,
father and mother.
Strange, some folks back home don't call to see
how you are doing,
But will do so, only, when they want something
They don't know if you are freezing, because you
don't have a good coat
Or from walking a long distance, your both feet hurt.
Some of them are living way better than us

If you don't send things for them, they make a big fuss
Mind you, they only want you to send them brand name
Which is not cheap, even when they are on sale.

Poor handymen and construction workers
They are exploited daily, by their unscrupulous employers
Sometimes they are so frustrated on a Friday,
All because, after working hard five days, they didn't get pay.
Along the way, there are some wonderful, caring employers
Who respect your judgment, with their sons and daughters
I was blessed, to take my son, to work with me
Something, I wouldn't forget, thanks, to the Keehn family.

Undocumented, we feel as though we are in a box
All we have is big dreams, behind those padlocks
They call us "illegal immigrants" I wonder why?
We make things happen here, I'm not telling a lie
We will never do some of these jobs, back in our country
Even though, no job is a disgrace, when done honestly.
Some get through with their papers in a short time frame
Others wait forever, wondering, when they will see home again.

To my brothers and sisters who have been waiting and waiting
Know for sure, your turn for the green card is coming
God knows exactly when it will come your way
In the meantime, give Him thanks and praise everyday

When you finally get those legal papers, in your hands
You cry tears of joy, knowing you can visit your homeland
You praise God for bringing you through, the long hard wait,
Landing a better job, with paid vacation, you so appreciate
I look back from where God has brought many of us from
The journey was tough and long for some
The sky is the limit, this for sure we know
No more stagnation in America

NOW, it is LEGAL immigrants' time to GROW.
March 1st 2016 -1-2 pm

Trini Christmas

Christmas time is here again
How I wished I was on a plane heading to Port -of -Spain
Where everyone is in high spirits, preparing
To have the place spic and span, come Christmas morning.
You can hear Daisy and Scrunter, playing loudly on the radio
As you sit writing postcards , and they begging you,
to low down de stereo
The balloons are in the bag, yuh not sure who blowing them up
Because last year, in your face a few of them did buss

From early December, folks love to ransack their place
Curtains down, chairs in a corner, make no mistake
Some folks are busy scrubbing and varnishing,
Late in the night , many trucks , are still delivering
Pots turn down, no time for cooking
Because ladder, Gazette paper, and paint brush,
are all over the kitchen
If people don't do that, to them it is not Christmas
By Christmas Eve night, that place will get back in order,
without a fuss.

Some are busy, scraping and painting
While others are making sure they get new curtains
Most men work from morning, till late in the evening
Because new cupboard, fridge and stove,
is needed for the kitchen
Everybody must have sweetbread ,
ginger beer and sorrel
If the wifee eh get enough money,
boy whole day she will quarrel
Mothers have the kids grinding fruits for the Black cake
With her pension, granny will buy a big pork leg, to bake

You must have apples and grapes, to give the little children
If you don't have any, they will talk 'bout you again.
People take their "sou sou" hand, in time for the holidays,
Buying new stuff, showing off,
just to hear what their neighbors would say.
Nice folks does be running and peeping , through their window,
When they see Courts truck stop, by people they know.
wondering how they will pay, for all them new things,
Because all year long, those same people, does be borrowing.

In every home ,there is excitement , on Christmas Eve night
Everyone wants their home, to look, just right.
The aroma of new plastic table cloth and vinyl for the floor
Does hit yuh nose, as you walk through the front door
In the back yard, ham is boiling in the Crix pan
But somebody have to sit there, and be the watchman
Otherwise when you go back out, your ham is gone
And that will make you really vex, all Christmas long.

Come Christmas morning, the place does look different ,
and smell so good,
Lunchtime, there is enough food ,to feed the whole neighborhood .
Macaroni pie, fresh pigeon peas, Callaloo , the works,
Evening time , you are so full, you can't even laugh at a joke.
Later, de parang side does pass, with bottle and spoon
If they drinking too much, you praying they would leave soon
When they gone, the well put away house , does be in ah mess
With all the singing and dancing, what do we expect?

There is no place to celebrate Christmas like back home
With plenty family and friends , you are NEVER alone
Pastel, roast pork, homemade bread and punch de crème
You can't wait for next year Christmas, to go back home again.
However , if you have to spend Christmas here in de cold,
Make the best of it , singing carols , from days of old.

Re-live those days, where Christmas in the island , is always sunny,
And you hear" SEASON GREETINGS "from even yuh enemy.

December 1st 2009

In Trinidad, I Remember When

I am amazed at how much times have changed
The experience I had back then, to switch it to now,
I will not trade
The lessons learned in my growing up days I cherish it dearly
The time these kids are growing up in, have them way too
spoiled and lazy.

Before we went to school we first had to do our chores
It could have been, sweeping the yard, making the bed
or hanging the towels over the doors
It was a time when kids had great respect for their elders
And your mother used to set her hair with pink sponge curlers.
I remember when we played dolly house and hide and seek.
Making a whole lot of noise laughing, and running all about, bare feet

I remember on Sundays and holidays only,
we drank Ovaltine and ate chicken.
I remember, while learning how to cook,
we also helped clean the kitchen
With breakfast, back then it was either, lime bud,
orange peel, fever grass, or some bush tea
Today we are so highfalutin we ordering,
large hazelnut and pumpkin coffee
Soaking Crix biscuits in your tea was something done regularly
It's a Trini thing ,done by a lot of families, and it so tasty.
I remembered taking my lunch in a rammed full
brown paper bag
By lunch time those hops bread would get very hard

Back then, there was nothing called a microwave
We had to warm up our food over the coal pot, in those days.
When you talk about pots of food, that was tasty and nice
My mother and grandmother's scrupulous cooking,

could have won them first prize
They prepared their many dishes from produce that they grow,
And would share these crops with people they don't even know .

I thought we were rich when we got a pitch oil stove with two burners.
That thing would sutt plenty, the food would taste smoky, when the
wick burned out in the center.
The whole house smelled, when they were making homemade bread
Which we ate with Blue Band butter, then after we went in our bed.

We tote water from the standpipe some distance from home
to do everything
In the barrel was water covered over, just for cooking ,
We washed our clothes with Breeze, in a wooden tub with
a jookin board.
And we never went to sleep, before saying our prayers
and thanking the Lord

Oh the days when Gazette, or should I say, newspaper,
was our Charmin, and Scott toilet paper
Thinking about those days back then, can surely make one
burst into laughter.
We had no comfortable toilet and bathroom with running water
We used an outhouse that was called a latrine, and some
galvanized put together, that was our shower.

The irons we had back then to press our clothes,
didn't work with electric.
We had to put them on top of the coal pot ,after they got very hot,
we wiped the bottom and that did the trick.
The two pitch oil lamps served as our electricity,
With seven of us on one bed, we were a close knit, happy family.

Thiefing milk, Milo and sugar, we all did while growing up
Even though when caught, we got licks, but we still didn't stop.
I remember saying , "I can't wait to work, to buy my own
milk, and Milo"
It's was a happy thought, every time I stepped into the
grocery store, called Hi-Lo.

Ladies and gentlemen it is good to look back, where
you came from
A little nostalgia, makes you appreciate God's blessings
for your own daughter and son
We must NEVER be ashamed of our tough humbled childhood,
that's our past.
Let us enjoy what we have with each other
All these memories are joyous, and in our heart they will last

June 1st, 2017

Love & Romance

Love

L is for love, a feeling we should demonstrate daily
O is for olive branch, we extend to others we hurt easily
V is for victory, we all have in Jesus Christ
E is for everlasting love, freely given without a price

February 2009

Junior

In April 2009, I attended a wedding
I lost a little weight and was looking slim
During the most wonderful cocktail hour
I met Joy and she introduced me to her debonair brother

He later told me, his name was Junior
Dressed in a nice suit, it was black in color
He was handsome, we sat at the same table
He wore no ring, I didn't know if he was available

We all sat there laughing and conversing
About ourselves, we were discussing
Joy then said "you better leave my brother alone"
But if I needed a ride, they will take me home".

We exchanged phone numbers, Junior and I
If he was married, I would not have wondered why
We took a few pictures and even moved on the dance floor
He was shaking his body, this man was no bore

We called each other occasionally
As for our friendship, it grew gradually
We went to a few movies and after had dinner
We talked about our jobs, he is a bus driver

I could go on writing but for now I will stop
Some information I just wouldn't drop
One thing bothers me, this brother does not like church
He is not a bandit, but I don't know which feels worst.

Serving the Lord is really important to me
Because he is the one who makes me free

I have made a few mistakes, here and there in the past
But I hope junior and my friendship will last and last.
                        October 18th 2009

Tribute to Pastor and Kathy Ann

A few years ago pastor went to Trinidad
His niece was running in Palo Seco and he was so glad
She was participating in a very important race
While there, pastor saw Kathy Ann's beautiful face

It was love at first sight ,he knew she would be his wife
He got back home and called her, morning, noon and night
Phone card after phone card, he paid a hefty price
This man really wanted this woman , in his life.

They got married July 29th 2006
Daily, God is blessing their relationship
This couple here is so full of joy
Together they have four girls and two handsome boys

Mr. and Mrs. Rojas are full of zest
As their love for each other is daily expressed
He pampers her, they are having a ball
There to help each other, if one slip or fall

Pastor and Sister Kathy Ann are a precious gem
On ICC members, they can always depend.
Their passion for life is oh so good
Their marriage is blessed, that's understood .

July 2008

Proposal

In my ear, I could hear my loud scream
This was only part of my dream
Yes I imagined a better life for myself
But never expected this beauty on the shelf
I didn't know a love like this existed
I will be your wife, there's going to be a wedding
You pop the question and I said" yes"
I'm very excited, I have to get a white dress.

Why

Why do you make me happy one minute
Why the next minute you can easily switch
After the hurtful insult you say you are sorry
And expect me to be ok, oh no,no baby

You and I

With loving eyes you look at me
With strong arms you protect me
With tender lips you kiss me
After whispering three POWERFUL words
" YOU LOVE ME"

Do you know I love you boy?
Do you know in every way, I show you how?
Do you know I'm happy to take care of you daily?
Do you know I need to be more than just your lady?

Where do we go from here?
Will it be the same way, year after year?
I am your lover and your friend
I promise to be with you till the end.
So what is stopping you from committing to me
I want to be yours legally
Just say the words, and I'll be your wife
Being your biggest support, the rest of my life
11/13/2016

Us

Have I wasted time being with you
What would you say, if you were in my shoe
In the beginning we were so happy
We were inseparable, in love, everyone could see

The many date nights after a hard day at work
Made us appreciate the moment, and our worth
Walking, holding hands, stealing a kiss
With you baby, those things I miss

Our passion produced beautiful offspring
Who I rocked to sleep while I smile and sing
Folks can't believe how much they look like both of us
They were birthed from our love, I don't see the fuss

I can't remember when things changed
What I did wrong to cause so much disdain
Your sweet words were no longer heard
Only demeaning insults that felt like fire burn

I take this experience as a lesson learned
I will not call it a mistake for I have grown
Learning to let go, and thanking you for setting me free
As I see the glass half full, not half empty
Saturday Sep.17th 2016

Thanks

Thanks for giving me this new day to see
Thanks for health and strength in my body
Thanks for taking good care of me
Thanks for loving me unconditionally

Thanks for the roof over my head
Thanks for sleep, on a comfortable bed.
Thanks for giving me eyes that see
Thanks for flowers and trees, they are nature's beauty

Thanks is a word I just can't stop using
Because you oh God have given me, so many blessings
It will take me forever to itemize them one at a time
I'm Saying thank you God, for EVERYTHING, and the sunshine.

Sunday November 20th 2016 - 9:30 am

Because

God has allowed you to celebrate another birthday.
You should thank Him
He has given you eyes to see, and a mouth to pray
You should love Him
He has provided for you, food, clothing and shelter.
You should worship Him
And because He is the Alpha and Omega
You should be happy to tell others about Him

Father

Father you are worthy, worthy to be praised
Father you are worthy, you're worthy to be praised
I give you all the glory, I give you all the praise
Father you are worthy
You're worthy to be praise
March 2010

God Our Friend

We had to memorize scripture verses for Sunday School
Against the enemy, we know it is our weapon, our tool
The Bible warned us to "guard our heart"
God is always with us, not far apart

The people who know God, shall be strong
With Him one can never go wrong
When we go to Jesus, He promises to give us rest
A rest that comes from God, he is the Best

When faced with situations God is right there
He will not give us, more than we could bear
His eyes are upon us constantly
Let's not forget to pray to Him daily
God knows exactly where we are and what we are going through
He said "even if you make your bed in hell, He is with you"

We have to have a relationship with God for ourselves
We can't depend on no one else
We need to use God's word to encourage others
Give a good word, to a sister brother or mother
We don't know what they are going through,
Sometimes a simple hello, or a smile is a good thing to do

Good Love

Love is a feeling I know I cannot hide
Love is a feeling I know I can't deny
It makes you excited even when things are down
With that love, it seems nothing can go wrong

I love, love
It's a feeling that only comes from above
God has deposited it into every one of us
In reality, it is so much better than lust

12/11/16

God's Presence

I may not live in a big mansion
But in my humble apartment, God is my foundation.
He guides and protects my home every day
As I continue to acknowledge Him in all my ways

He Cares

Even though we've messed up time and time again
Lord you prove to us, You are our friend
When things look bad, from our point of view
Your Word reminds us, to keep our eyes on You
We know serving You, is the best thing to do
When we feel blue, Lord you'll help us through
On this their birthday, they'll show their love for You
Because you changed their hearts, and made them new.

God's Word was given for our good
And we are to obey
Not choose the verses we like best,
Then live it our own way

I Am

Do you know who I am, do you, do you?
I am washed by the Blood of the Lamb
I accepted the Lord in 1993
Serving and worshipping Him, I can do so freely

Yesterday is history, it has come and gone
You made some mistakes, and did a few wrong
Through it all, God has made you strong
In His arms is where you belong

Daily declaring that God is your king
In Him you live and move and have your being
Thank Him for allowing you to see another year
Praise Him because He hasn't given you a spirit of fear

Fear

God can meet all of your needs
You must believe in order to receive
Don't be discouraged walk with your head held high
Because God almighty, is always by your side

ICC *Anniversary*

Today we all came to ICC,
To celebrate , the 21st anniversary
Some came from near, some came from far
Getting here by walking, flying, bus or motor car

If you want to hear a good word please come to ICC
Not only is the pastor an author, he is also a Trini
Two decades ago , he started this powerful ministry
Preaching around the world, he is loved by everybody.

2010

Jesus is

Jesus is the way the truth and the life
Trust Him my friend, and He'll make everything right
We must acknowledge Him in all our way
And definitely we are going to have better days
The battle is not ours, it is the Lord's
Leave all things to Him, He is Almighty God

As we begin to move with God, the enemy is grieved
When we worship God , our Father is well pleased
We know Jesus will always be our friend
His unconditional love, will never end

We ask God to create in us a clean heart
As we look to the future, and let go of the past
Praying should not be an inconvenience
Because victorious living, we all want to experience

Remember

Remember, you can't put all your trust in a friend
Sometimes they turn their back, just when you need them
Although they promised to be there to the end
Only on Christ Jesus you can depend

Remember, God's mercy never comes to an end
On His love you can always depend
Even if your faith is small as a mustard seed
God can supply every one of your needs

Remember, whatever you are hoping for, keep the faith
It may not come right away, and you may have to wait
It will never come when it is too late
God knows when to deposit it, at your gate

Remember to be thankful for the things in your life
Your son, daughter, husband or wife
We want the Lord to always bless us
But to keep all his commandments, we make a fuss

2009

Tithing

We need to pay our tithes, that's what God asks
Some of us do it, as though it is a task
If we want God's blessings to come our way
Why don't we start paying our tithes every Sunday

We can't stop tithing, because we have bills to pay
Do what God's word says and He will make a way
We can't outgive God, no matter how we try
He'll do the impossible, our eyes will open wide

We pay for our utilities, credit card and food
Yet we so easily, break this, our Father's rule
We rob God when we hold our tithes back
We are hurting ourselves, and that's a fact

Rent, clothing, all our needs God will supply
When we pay our tithes, we will not have to cry
No matter how much we feel, we could pray
Until we start tithing, we would not fully, see our way

We sometimes wonder where our salary went
Because, before we wink, we don't have a cent
Let us pay our tithes religiously
And the windows of heaven will open immediately.

All God asks is for ten percent.
But we keep it back to buy clothes and shoes
to make some movements
If we want Him to keep us, from harm and danger
Then we must do what he asks, my brother and my sister

We feel we need our whole week's pay
To take better care of our family everyday
If we refuse to pay our tithes, many things will go wrong,
No matter how much we pray, or sing gospel songs.

Listen to me, I learned the hard way
Be excited about paying tithes, starting today
In our lives, God will do miracle after miracle
He is God, and He is more than able.

10/30/2009

What Do You Have?

What do you have in your hand?
Is it small or is it grand
What do you have in your home
Will you share with others, or have it alone?
What do you have in your purse
Can you share it, things won't get worst
What do you have in your pocket
You can keep all to yourself, or you can share it
Whatever you have, it is God who supplies
He is our God, your provider, He is El Shaddai.

10/25/09

God's Word

To obey is better than sacrifice
If you don't you'll pay a price
God wants us to obey His every word
A request made, to every man, woman, boy or girl
God's word is a lamp unto my feet
Today you look so nice and sweet
Have a little to drink and plenty to eat

ICC *Mortgage Burning*

In 1999, served with eviction, our church had to move
With little money in hand, we, didn't know what to do
We had to locate a building, immediately
Pay attention to me, here's the story, of ICC's journey

Finding a vacant building, was in Pastor Rojas' hand
Knowing his taste, we expected somewhere grand
When he finally brought us, to see this place
Every member had a shocked look on their face

Akini couldn't believe it, he passed the place straight
He had the address, but thought, "there must be a mistake"
Dirty oiled stained walls, garbage, the place was a mess
But we prayed, and were determined, to make here the best.

With working tools in hands, that Saturday morning
Demolishing the roof, were Pastor, Devina, Brian, and Harrigain
Anika, Pat, Cindy, Abby, Allison and Candace
Were all busy, carrying out bags, and bags, of garbage

For the renovation, everyone wanted to contribute
Some days the ladies even cooked the men, cowheel soup
There were days they ate macaroni pie, Callaloo and stew chicken
Cooked with love, from Hazel's small kitchen

Pelau, fried rice and peanut punch
Were some of the dishes the men also got for lunch
Marcia and Mary, made a wicked ice tea
While Petal did an outstanding job, as secretary

Many members came in the evening, after work
This place started to take form, the brothers didn't make joke

Parker, Andrew, Randy and Brother Ken
Called themselves," ICC iron men"

Even though we had no heat, and the place was very cold
Many worked tirelessly in coats, to achieve our goal
Nonstop, work went on here, every single day
But on Friday nights, we all stopped to pray

Thanks to Brother Harrison, Ralph, Abdon , Kelvin and Andrew
For being a part of the ICC building crew
Not forgetting David, Michelle, Faith and Mohammed
All the electrical work, was done by Anthony Ifill

Finally the building was completed, that was a celebration
In May 2000, we had a fabulous dedication
Gloria Harrigain, sewed these beautiful drapes
Recently she went to meet the Lord, oh how our hearts ache

When we reflect, on how this place used to be
We take pride in saying," we helped build ICC"
Some have moved away, and no longer fellowship here
But their calls, on and off, show they love and care

If you are here, and your name I forgot to mention
Please don't hold it against me, it was not my intention
With God's blessings we are now mortgage free
From an old rundown bus garage, to a church called ICC
Where everyone is treated like family

Yes, the mortgage is paid off, because of the hard work you do
Today, we are happy you came back, and we say, thank you
There is plenty food, & drinks, no we are not serving wine
But we are sure to share great memories, and have a good time

7/31/13

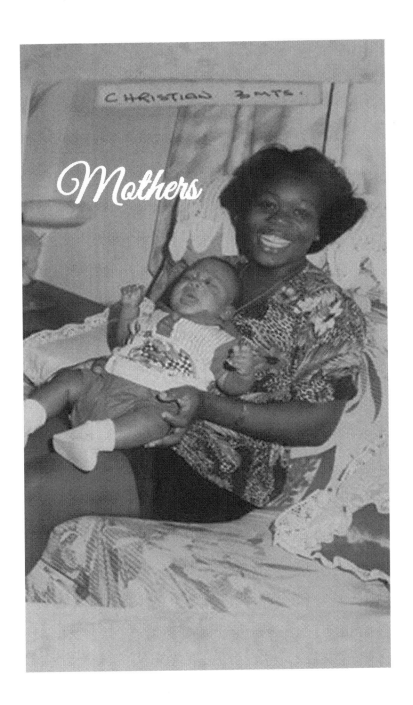

Mothers

1 A mother loves her child the moment she know she is pregnant
Taking special care , she wants to be a good parent
As the weeks turn to months she's anxious to deliver her baby
Breast feeding and multitasking, she's such a proud mommy

2 A mother is someone created for the role
Whether she is a mom of a baby boy, or a pretty little girl
She nurtures her children like no one else can
Sometimes doing it all by herself , without the presence of a man

3 Twenty four seven, we can call on our mother
When others say no, she'll always give us a soft answer
When we do wrong, yes she uses the rod of correction
Even though she dislikes being the one, in that situation

4 Without moms , where would we be?
Whether she's a Grenadian, American, Bajan or Trini
A mother's love is unconditional
The sacrifices she makes are so many to mention

5 . Yes A mother loves her children , unconditionally
She will do almost anything, to take care of her " pickney"
She wakes up early, long before the sunrise
Preparing meals sometimes with little sleep, oh how she sacrifice
Cleaning and washing in one day that is what she does
The tasty meals she prepares is cooked with so much love
She mends clothing even though she's not a seamstress
Taking time to care for her kids, she's such a princess

6 . Mothers are a good role model and a good counselor
She's well qualified, even though she wasn't taught by a professor

No manual is given, after giving birth at the hospital
It's trial and error, in the beginning,
mothers got so much potential
All by themselves sometime mothers raise the babies
The kids grow up respectful and loving,
even though sometimes no help from daddy
She is up late cleaning , after dinner and home work
Getting good grades is a must, because mothers don't make joke

7 . Her sleep, her time, she gives up freely for her children
Making sure they grow up, not to be society's problem
Scrubbing , shopping , cleaning, yes she does it with pride
When kids disappoint them, mothers are sad and sometimes cry
They take care of every one without complaining
Mothers deserves a trophy, she's a champion
Caregiver, provider she wears many hats
She's your biggest supporter, that's a fact
She's a doctor, teacher, designer and friend
In another life I want my mother, to be my mom again

8 . Mother still finds time to take care of herself
Dressing nicely in the latest trend
She's stylish , effervescent, oh so cool
As she hugs her kids daily before they leave for school
Thank you mom, for teaching us right from wrong
Thank for your tolerating us, and reminding us to always be strong.
Thanks for allowing us to be who we are
You are our champion
Thanks for always, being in our corner mother.

May 2010

Mother's Day Birthday

It's nice to celebrate a birthday
Around the same time as Mother's Day
For mothers are the best
They stand out from among the rest
Cooking, cleaning, they do it all
And bounce right back from every fall
Hip hip hooray , one year older and wiser
We thank God for all the birthday mothers

May 2009

Let's Celebrate

My Godmother, Nenny's Birthday

Happy birthday, my godmother Vilma
This is coming from your awesome God daughter
You have also been a second mother to me
Vilma Lewis, I love you so so dearly

You are a mother of four boys and two girls
I wish I could give you the whole wide world
You gave birth to six children, I was your adopted one
Being at your home was so much fun

From my first vacation day at your home at age eleven
I tasted your food and felt like I was in heaven
Diamonds and pearls I'd love to give you
Loving you continuously, I'll forever do

Richard and Merlene taught me to ride a bicycle
I loved going with you to Penal, Siparia and Palo Seco
Nenny, you really are an amazing cook,
I love your baked chicken , pelau and pigtail soup

Mr. Lewis, your husband, openly welcomed me
Even though we called his car names , like Mumblee
I love that Merlene and I share the same birthday
For long life and health, for you I always pray

Nenny I write this poem with tears in my eyes
Wishing I was sitting right by your side
But since I'm in New York, and you in Trini
I will say it to you again, happy birthday, I love you Nenny

2013

Michelle

Happy birthday Michelle
Girl, You really do your job very well
Today is your birthday and you like, drinking coffee
Don't study your co-host, you are not crazy
You are a boss when it comes to baking
Cheese cake, black cake, punch de crème, anything
Your birthday indeed should be your day off
But you showed up for work, cause you love your job of course
Next year please God, let Sherry work and you stay home
Leaving the ice man, in the studio all alone
You and Rennie B make an awesome team
He is a legend, you are a queen
May God's blessings continue to surround you
In everything you plan, say or do
                    4/13/16

Alana's 40th Birthday

We are all gathered here today,
Because, my niece, is celebrating her 40th birthday.
Alana Francisca Bourne is her name
For keeping her healthy and strong, Almighty God, gets the fame.

Alana is a friend, aunt and daughter,
To Abby and Kevin, she is their big sister.
Toni is proud to call this fine lady, mommy,
They are all part of the fun loving, Bourne family.

Alana was born, to Faith and Sharkie, on a Holy Thursday,
A cutie-pie, from day one, please, listen to what I say.
April 15 1976, she came into this world.
The new addition to the Bourne clan was this beautiful girl.

From a kid, Alana was always full of love,
She will rather give you a hug, instead of a shove.
Mammy was so glad to have Alana as her first grandchild,
When she is around, Alana makes us all smile.

I carried Alana with me, everywhere I went,
Even though in my teens, sometimes I didn't have a cent.
I would take her to spend time with her godmother Christine,
Who dressed Alana nicely, and treated her like a little queen.

Alana attended Batie's preschool, at age four,
Always waving goodbye, when she reached the school door.
Later, she headed to La Puerta Government School,
Where she studied hard, because she didn't want to be a fool.

From there, my girl went to Diego Martin Sec.
Alana treats her elders with kindness and respect
She left school, with a full certificate,
Her passion for life, we so appreciate.

Growing up, Alana was considered an introvert
Laughing ladylike, at my sometimes, funny jokes
I didn't even know this child could have wine and get on badly
Seeing Alana in that light, for us, was a shocking reality,

Alana continues to strive for greatness daily,
She perseveres with every step, no if or maybe.
From an adorable baby, Alana developed into a pretty teenager,
From a gorgeous teen, she became an awesome mother.

During Divali, Alana, dresses like a true Indian in a Sari,
For Halloween, this girl can transform to look so scary.
Dressing up and looking good, with my niece, is so apparent,
Can't believe, almost fifteen years ago Alana became a parent.

I am so proud and honored, to be Alana's aunt,
Disliking her for any reason, I absolutely can't
She allowed me, to fulfill my greatest desire,
Witnessing Toni's birth, made my love for her stronger.

When it comes to being late, Alana takes the whole darn cake
She never rushes for anything, work, party or even a date,
She boasts, she is never late, everyone else is always early
Alana must be living in a dream, or she is really, really crazy
If you want her to be on time, give her an advance of four hours
You may still have a little wait, its Alana, so don't dig any horrors

Everyone looks amazing in your beautiful white outfits
The way you put yourself together, you look absolutely rich
There is plenty to snack and yes plenty liquor to drink
Please don't get drunk and vomit in the people sink

Let us enjoy this moment, because life is so very short,
Mingle with each other, dance and wine of course.
Yes, we will eat, drink and be merry,
I hope Alana have enough food, for everybody.

Alana girl, tonight we salute you,
For achieving everything, you put your mind to.
Concerning your future dreams, may they all come true,
As God's blessings continue to surround you.
                  Wednesday March 24 2016. 7am

Happy Birthday

Whether you celebrate your birthday in November or December
You want it to be a day you will always remember
If you are turning fifteen, thirty-five or fifty one
Enjoy your birthday, have lots of fun

Birthday Poem

Brothers and sisters, it is birthday time
Let us see, who will stand in line
If you are celebrating a birthday this week
I want you please, to stand on your feet
This place is wonderful because you are in the world
Please come forward, boy or girl
Stand up by the altar, don't be afraid
We wouldn't ask your age, only your name
I know, some of you were born, in the 1960's
That means this year, you turn plenty
You are looking good, as we all can see
Clap your hands, if you agree with me
Long ago folks used to hide their age
Now today, some are very brave
Maybe you're wondering, why I'm talking so long
Watch our birthday folks, they are looking so young

June 2009

Another Birthday Poem

Hip hip hip, hooray
Today wonderful people are having a birthday
Some of them are very young
And they are feeling very strong
Then there are those who are a little older
They are full of life, and so much wiser
Whether they are one, nine, thirty-five or seventy
Keep trusting the Lord , and blessings you will see
Everyone loves to celebrate their birthday
But some, their age they would never say
Your age, we would like to know
Whatever it is, I know it doesn't show

Amanda's Birthday

Happy birthday Amanda
You are Anna's precious daughter
Every day of the year
May you get some grey hair
I hope you enjoy your day
What else you expect me to say
You are an only child
Today it is okay if you behave wild
    12/06/16-8:30 am

Baby Shower

We are all gathered here in this beautifully decorated hall
To celebrate and have a ball
Broderick and Marcus are having a baby
They are going to be happy, no if's or maybe
Ten fingers and toes and a cute little nose
Mommy and Daddy their excitement shows

March nineteenth, two thousand and seventeen
Baby will be a prince, because mom is a queen
There is plenty of delicious food to eat
Move around and dance, don't stay in your seat
There is also a variety of things to drink
But PLEASE don't get drunk and vomit in the people sink

With gifts in hands, we will express
Mom to be, your shower will be the BEST
This day is filled with so much joy
Broderick and Marcus are having a boy

From morning till night, we will wonder
If baby prince will look like his mother or father
This baby will be so much fun
No time for the gym, he will have mom on the run

Yes, they already have the baby's name
Broderick girl, your life will never be the same
Marcus man, your son, you will adore
People please, don't mess up the floor

Thank you all for coming today
Look at mom and dad, they don't know what to say

Let us eat, drink and have a good time
Every one of you here is looking mighty fine.

Susan's Wedding

This is what I have to say about Susan Bhola
She's a new wife, a sister, friend and daughter
When you are around her, you cannot feel blue
Especially when you see the monologues, she can do

There's so much I could share about this young lady
She's articulate, sassy, dramatic and oh so, funny
A very powerful, serious, woman of God
With all her heart, Susan loves the Lord.

We became good friends, many years ago,
When after church she offered me, a sweet ripe mango
Up to this day, l never had a mango sweet like that
Susan really knows how to pick the sweet ones from the rack

Along with others, we enjoyed pepper shrimp and scrabble.
On Tuesday nights, at my dining table.
Many times we stayed up chatting , until very late
Talking and testifying how "God is great"

If you ever need a mighty prayer partner,
You can always call this woman from Siparia
This girl is a true prayer warrior,
She could even make satan accept Jesus, as Lord and savior

Mrs. Girard is now your married name,
For blessing you with this amazingly patient man, God gets the fame
Calvin knew you were worth waiting for,
As the weeks turned to months, his love grew more and more

I am overly excited Susan, on this your wedding day
The best of everything to you and your husband, I pray
May God grant you both, all your hearts' desire
Blessing your awesome love and commitment to each other

Congratulations my friend, I am very happy for you
Prince William & Kate's love, ain't want nothing with you two
I wish you joy, peace and happiness,
As God continues daily to bless this wonderful relationship.

January 25th 2014

Christmas Time

For Christmas

This holiday I was looking for a perfect gift for you
It turned out to be the hardest thing to do
What can I give to someone who has everything
A book, household items, perfume , Lord I can't think
So I decided to give to you something that is priceless
It will make you smile, and you wouldn't have to guess
I am sending you this little poem that I've written with love
Full of blessings and good wishes from above.

12/21/16-5:05am

New Year Thanks

My mind is racing with numerous things I have to do
But the most important one is to stop and say "thank you"
As the old year quickly vanishes away
The excitement of a New Year, is just a few days
Thanking you for a whole year of making my car payments
And also for being able , to pay my rent

December 28 2016 - 10am

Pastor Rojas

We are honoring our pastor in a very special way
Lucien Clarie Rojas is his name
For keeping and blessing him, God gets the fame

At the age of seventeen, he accepted the Lord
In a little Baptist church, he answered God's call
He ran to the altar with tears in his eyes
In a river in Moruga, he was baptized

Glad for her son, his mother prepared Sunday food
But being filled with the Holy Spirit, he was in no mood
Callaloo, stew chicken and macaroni pie
Lucien couldn't eat, mommy couldn't understand why

At age nineteen, he started to preach,
Sharing the gospel to those he could reach

He spent many days, praying and fasting
Assisting his pastor, he was a great blessing

With four smooth tires, he sold his motor car
To gather money for his trip to America
Dressed in Long Johns at Piarco Airport
He was wet with sweat, pacing back and forth

Pastor Rojas, we meet to honor you
Full of gratitude for the work that you do
You are a husband, father, pastor and friend
God has called you to be a fisher of men

Pastor Rojas -ICC Journey

From Cachipe Village in Moruga
Lucien Rojas migrated to America
On May 18th nineteen ninety two
He wanted something meaningful to do
He got into ministry, today he's the pastor of ICC

In a tiny living room, on Kingston Avenue
He started the ministry, with just a few
As the weeks quickly turned into months
The few members became a very big bunch

Pastor Rojas continued seeking God's face
Then moved the ministry to Lincoln Place
The members were growing every week.
So he relocated to East 21st Street

From East 21st Street, to East New York Avenue
That store front too, we soon outgrew
God blessed us here on 1673 Dean Street
The place was a mess, now it is so sweet

After two decades pastor preached around the world,
But remained a gem to every boy and girl
His sense of humor, one always remembers
To the members, he is our spiritual father

The trials came and lasted a bit long
Through it all, pastor, you stood strong
Even when the times were tough
You never quit and, said "you've had enough"

God kept you for over 20 years
He'll do it again, so have no fear
You've sat and passed the entire test
God isn't finished with ICC yet.

Pastor Rojas, we all salute you
As God's work, you continue to do
God is good all the time
Continue my pastor, to shine, shine, shine
                    April 4th 2009
                  To God be the glory

P A N A *President*

P A N A wanted someone reliable, hardworking,
honest and efficient
To represent their many churches, as President
They considered a few well abled individuals, to fill the post
Later, they unanimously voted Lucien Rojas,
because he stood out the most.
That is why, we all came here today from various locations
To witness this special but different inauguration
Yes, the president is none other than the pastor of ICC
Who is short in stature, funny, and a born Trini

In Trinidad ,he was known as the mighty chicken
Because calypso in his early years he used to sing
Even though he stutters at times, he gets the job done
When pastor is around, you are sure to have fun

At the age of seventeen, he accepted the Lord
In a little Baptist church, he answered God's call
He ran to the altar with tears in his eyes
In a river in Moruga, he was baptized

Glad for her son his mother prepared Sunday food
But being filled with the Holy Spirit, he was in no mood
Callaloo, stew chicken, rice and macaroni pie
Lucien couldn't eat, his mom couldn't understand why

At age nineteen, he started to preach,
Sharing the gospel to those he could reach
He spent many days, praying and fasting
Assisting his pastor, he was a great blessing

With four smooth tires, he sold his motor car
To gather money for his trip to America
Dressed in Long Johns at the hot Piarco Airport
He was wet with sweat, pacing back and forth

On May 18th nineteen ninety two
He wanted something meaningful to do
He knew he had to get back into ministry,
Today he's the proud pastor of ICC

Lucien Clarie Rojas, we meet to support you
Full of gratitude for the great work that you do
You are a husband, father, friend and author
To the list of things you are , we now add !
President of PANA.

                        1/28/17- 7pm

Tribute to Karen Garcia

On May 31st, nineteen sixty something
A baby girl was born, with a voice to sing
Karen Cheryl Dickson was her name
When she accepted the Lord,
Her life was never the same

She joined ICC in two thousand and one
She sang at a concert, it was so much fun
She got involved in various ministries
With great joy, she did them effortlessly

In two thousand and seven, she entered a contest
And proved to the judges, she was the best
Out of twelve contestants , she came in first
Her euphoric voice, stood out the most

Sunday after Sunday, worship she led
God is alive He is not dead
When it comes to the things of God,
She is very serious
She gives to Him, her very best

While cleaning the church and dusting the chairs
God was preparing a husband for her named Richard
They got married right here at ICC
It is bitter sweet to see Karen leave

We really hate to see you go
But your husband ,your head, you must follow
Don't let anything or anyone deter you
From what God has called you to do

Karen you will be an asset, where you will fellowship
May God continue to bless your relationship
Singer, mother, wife and friend
At ICC we will welcome you, again and again...

Bon Voyage Jevon

A fine young man whose name is Jevon
Knew he was blessed from the day he was born
He stands close to six feet tall
To some of his peers, they look really small
He has to go away for a little while
So we want to send him off in style
We at ICC will miss you very much
Because for over a year you will not be with us

We really hate to see you go
And pray your procedure will move fast and not slow
Pack your bags don't make a fuss
When the time is right you will come back in a rush
Jevon's sisters, Candace and Petal, love him very much
They pray that God will bless, whatever his hands touch
He is a son, brother and a friend
Jevon remember only on God, you can depend

New friends in Trinidad, you are sure to make
Let them know how much you like chicken and steak
You love the Lord, he is your guide
Tell others about him, with joy and pride
While over there, God will be with you
Seek Him first, in all you do
He will protect and keep you while you are there
Remember he has not given you a spirit of fear.

Bon voyage to our sweet Jevon
In Trini, boy, you will have lots of fun
For Christmas this year, you will be in the sun
While up here from the snow we will have to run

Farewell My Neighbour

Saying farewell is never easy to do
Especially when a couple, has grown on you
I love these people, their leaving is making me blue
I can't get another neighbor, who could stand in their shoe

Three years ago, I met Mr. & Mrs. Thomas.
We developed a friendship, forever it will last,
A few months ago, they told me they were moving,
My heart sank, I hoped they were joking

Joan and Clinton, I'll miss you terribly
I have your number, I will call regularly
I hope my singing didn't drive you away
I'll stop it now, if you'll change your mind and stay

As the months quickly turned into days,
They began packing, to be on their way.
In my kitchen stands their gift, I greatly appreciate
Writing this poem is heart breaking, make no mistake.

Coming up the stairs will now feel very different,
Especially, Joan's early morning cooking,
I will miss the scent
Sharing our meals, was a way of showing we care,
I always felt safe & secure, because they were there.

I'll miss the alert calls when there's an emergency
Mr. Thomas made sure things were resolved, immediately.
They looked out for us, in more ways than one,
Losing them as my neighbors, will not be fun.
Bon voyage Mr. and Mrs. Thomas, enjoy your new home
With God by your side, you'll never be alone. *05/20/13*

Ms. Johnson

Congratulation on your new accomplishment.
In the OMH food service department
This promotion, it is a gift from God
Walk in my sister, this is your reward.
Even though I've known you, for only a few months.
We talk about God's goodness, while we have lunch.
Continue to trust Him, yes indeed, He loves you
Acknowledge Him, in all that you do.

The road ahead may have some twists and turns
With help from your seniors, they'll make sure you learn.
Promotion comes from God, not from man
You will do an excellent job, "yes you can"

Ms. Johnson, continue to stand on God's word
His pay back, is much better than gold
You were chosen, because you passed the test
God chose you because He knew you were the best

There will be changes, you will have to make
Some may not like it, still give God praise.
No man can curse, who God has blessed
Do not be afraid, God is with you Janet.

September 17th 2010

Thank You KPC

Saying goodbye is never easy
I'm saying it today, to Ms. Wheeler, Johnson , Pringles and Mc Ketty
Every beginning has an end
At KPC I made quite a few friends.

In 2010, I started working here
Full of faith, but I must say 'a little fear'
I'm glad I started as a food service worker
It's here I met Jennifer, Forde, Scott, Lucky, Kassie and Glover

Days later, I met Ms. Wheeler,
She introduced me to B. Johnson, Kerney, Howard and Doranda
I learned a lot working on the cold station
While getting along with others from different nations

The weeks turned to months, months into years
I mastered all my tasks without fear
All endings have new beginning
I am sad to be leaving, I will miss Bernard singing.

Thanks to the morning staff for embracing me.
Working with Brown and Clarke was not easy
Their critique made me so much stronger
It was all fun, with lots of laughter

To those, whose names I didn't mention
Keep up the good work, as you perfect your station
The laughter, and camaraderie, I will surely miss
I am moving on, God has granted me, my wish.
I will not miss working the overtime shift, it was a sacrifice
Or cutting pans of cheese cake, slice by slice. 10/07/2012

Joanne

Some people don't know, what it's like, to have a friend
Someone on whom, for sure, you can depend
I know of a person, who fits this role
We have been friends, since we were five years old.
Joanne Cheryl Bridgewater is her name
For keeping her healthy and strong, Almighty God gets the fame.
Joanne is always pleasant to be around
God's word keeps her standing, on solid ground .

To Shirley and Neville Bridgewater
Joanne is the first of their four daughters
Sherry Ann and Nicole also adopted me as a sister and friend
Then Shelly came on the scene and more love was given to me again
The Bridgewaters are strongly bonded because of unity
The love I have for them, started immediately
I know I have a mother in Miss Shirley
She always treats me, like I'm part of the family

Joanne Bridgewater knows what she is all about
She is soft spoken, and yes, I have a big mouth
Our personalities are unique cause we are so opposite
Yet we share this beautiful and amazing friendship
After primary school we never lost contact
We always, no matter the distance, had each other's back.
Different secondary schools couldn't stop our visiting each other
Joanne was loved , by Cynthia ,my mother.

I spent many weekends and Christmas, at their humble home
I thought they were rich cause they had a washing machine
and a telephone
Love is what this family is really rich with
Being around them, I never felt home sick.

We played and ran around like crazy, in the yard
Leaving them to go back home , used to be so hard
Miss Shirley was amazing, she gave us space to create things
We made some *delicious* sweetbread from scratch, in her kitchen
While there, I learned to eat with a knife and fork
It was uncomfortable in the beginning, but I mastered it, of course.

Joanne is so calm , she'll never suffer with high blood pressure
When she prays, my friend indeed, is a prayer warrior
She supports me in more ways than one
To my only child Christian, he is, her godson.
I still have the gold chain Joanne gave to me
In 1996, when I was migrating to another country
In my purse, is a passage of Scripture
She blessed me with, to help shape my future

Joanne never judged me, her compassion never stopped
Helping me out of the drain at age nine,
when an Indian girl beat me up.
The girl said she had enough of my bullying
And that day she was determined to show me something
Thank you Jo for holding my hands
as we walked up Green Street
Dusting off the moss of my clothes and laughing
at my wet dirty feet
Having lunch, sitting at home, or spending a day at the mall
Whatever we do, we always have a ball

Through the good or bad times, Jo was always there for me
When I almost hit rock bottom, she showed up unexpectedly
She took me driving in her brand new Charmant motorcar
I don't consider her a friend, she is my sister
Daily I pray, for God's continued guidance in her life
"Keeping her Lord, from adversity and strife"
May He guide her, as she moves around every bend

Joanne Cheryl Bridgewater, is my best friend to the end
May 1, 2016

Thanks Martha & Jane

Saying goodbye is never easy to do
Especially when a family, has grown on you
I love these people, I am saying it bold
Knowing them, is much better than gold

I attended an interview at their home in July 2002
Babysitting and cooking, were some things I had to do
That day I met Martha, Jane And Marilyn
From Patsy a former employee, I was highly recommended

In the beginning I was extremely nervous
I sang and did my chores, they never made a fuss
I later met Hunter who was away in college
A young man so nice and bursting with knowledge

The daily handwritten notes, I looked forward to
It gave me instructions on the things I had to do
I did my job with pride each day
They trusted my judgments and never stood in my way

When my mom passed away, they were there for me
Then I got sick, and Martha took me to the emergency
When Christian was in the hospital for over six weeks
Their love and support, kept me on my feet

Seven and a half years later, I am moving on
This family is unique, that's why I stayed so long
I will miss them, but this is not where it ends
They are no longer my boss, but now my good friends

April 30th 2010

Zita Wilson

Zita Wilson, was a wife, a friend, and a mother,
She gave birth to four handsome sons, and a gorgeous daughter
Unfortunately on January 26th, she passed away ,
Leaving not a dry eye, at her bedside, that day.

Zita was loved by everybody,
She treated everyone, like they were family .
She was sometimes funny but very feisty ,
If you mess with her kids, she wouldn't take it lightly.

Zita had a plaster for every sore ,
Don't try to hurt her, she promise she'll break the law.
This woman was small in stature, but powerful with mouth ,
She loved her grandchildren, without a doubt .

Mom loved to dress and always looked elegant,
From talking with her kids, she was a no nonsense parent.
Don't ask her to stay home, if you are dressing to go out,
She'll give you a tongue lashing, with her saucy , hot mouth.

She liked to be a part of a real, good lime,
Especially playing mas with All Stars, at carnival time.
Even though she walked with a cane, you couldn't stop Zita
She'll walk and dance the longest distance, it didn't matter

She chose the carnival season, to say goodbye ,
This is one of her favorite times , so don't ask why.
From the first day I met her, she welcomed me with open arms,
Warning me with one finger ,she said
" you better don't do my Junior no harm"

She treated me, with love and respect ,
With my mother in law, "*what you see, is what you get*"
Being around her, I always felt comfortable
We had many long chats, sitting by my dining table .

She embraced my family , and even my friends
Sadly after today, we will not be seeing her again
Mom, you are going to be missed by all,
I know in heaven, you are having a ball
I don't know a mother in law, who could stand in your shoe
Sleep tight in God's arms, WE LOVE YOU .
Wednesday 27th January 2016 11:pm

Goodbye Alicia

Alicia was a mother, sister and my best friend
On May 12th her precious life came to an end
Even though my best friend has passed away
In my heart forever she will stay

When the doctor gave her the sad news, she called me crying
I could not believe what I was hearing
As the weeks turned to months, her faith in God grew
Keeping the faith to the last, that much is true

When I got a new job, she was happy as can be
"the sky is the limit Hazee", that's what she said to me
Throughout her ordeal she maintained a positive outlook
Fighting till the end, with every strength it took
Thank you Alicia for being my friend
Thank you for being one, right down to the end
Thank you for the many nights of playing scrabble
While eating corn and pepper shrimp at my dining table

Thank you for loving me for who I am
Thanks for always lending, a helping hand
Thank you for being there when my first child died
Thanks for wiping my eyes, the many months I cried

When I had a problem Alicia was always there for me
Her love and support kept me on my feet
Words can't describe what a big heart she had
Always giving of her best and lending a helping hand

When she corrected my misspelled words, boy I would be mad
"I'm a teacher "she'd say, and we'd both laugh out hard
Teaching was her passion, her students will miss her

So would her children, Adrian, Jayden And Akia

I didn't know today I'll be saying goodbye to you
Alicia this is not easy, it is a hard thing for me to do
I don't have another friend, who can stand in your shoe
Sleep in God's arms my best friend, "I love you"
May 13th 2010

Glossary

Breeze	A brand of laundry detergent
Blue Band butter	Popular brand of Butter used Trinidad and Tobago in the old days
Bottle and Spoon	Used as instruments against glass to make music
Callaloo	A type of soup made in Trinidad and Tobago
Coal pot	Clay cooking pot fueled by coals
Crix biscuits	Popular Trinidad and Tobago Crackers
Cut tail	A beating
Daisy	Popular parang singer, now deceased
Dolly house	A doll's house
Gazette	Trinidad and Tobago newspaper, now obsolete
Highfalutin	Pompous or pretentious.
Hi-Lo	Trinidad and Tobago Grocery store chain, now called Massy Stores
Hops bread	A flaky dinner roll
ICC	International Christian Center
Jookin board	A board or frame having a corrugated surface to wash clothes.
Licks	A beating
MHTA	Mental Health Therapy Aide
Milo	A chocolate and malt powder drink that can be drunk hot or cold
Moruga	A remote village on the central south coast of Trinidad
OMH	Office of Mental Health
Ovaltine	A chocolate and malt powder drink that can be drunk hot or cold
Parang	A popular Spanish folk music originating from Venezuela and Trinidad and Tobago
Pelau	A popular Trinidad and Tobago dish made with rice, pigeon peas and meat

Pickney	A child.
Pigtail soup	A spicy soup made with split peas, pigtail and provision
Pitch oil lamps	A lamp fueled by pitch oil. Pitch oil is Kerosene or paraffin oil
Pitch oil stove	A stove fueled by pitch oil. Pitch oil is Kerosene or paraffin oil
Punch de crème	A milk drink similar to eggnog comprised of sweet milk, eggs and rum
Scrunter	The name of a popular calypsonian
Sorrel	Dark red drink with a raspberry like flavor; made from the petals of the sorrel plant
Sou sou	A form of rotating savings and credit association; a type of informal savings club arrangement between a small group of people. The basic principle is that each member of the group makes a standard contribution to a common fund once per time period.
Sandpipe	An outdoor pipe used as a communal water supply for neighborhoods which lack individual housing water service.
Sutt	Soot
Thiefing	Stealing
Tote	Carry
Trini	A native of Trinidad ; Trinidad

If you would like to contact Hazel
please visit her website.

www.hazelbourne.com

47825273R00080

Made in the USA
Middletown, DE
03 September 2017